Llewellyn's Va

G000154584

The Truth About

NUMEROLOGY

by David Allen Hulse

Author of

The Key of It All

Llewellyn Publications is the oldest publisher of New Age Sciences in the Western Hemisphere. This book is one of a series of introductory explorations of each of the many fascinating dimensions of New Age Science—each important to a new understanding of Body and Soul, Mind and Spirit, of Nature and humanity's place in the world, and the vast unexplored regions of Microcosm and Macrocosm.

Please write for a full list of publications.

1993
Llewellyn Publications
P.O. Box 64383-395, St. Paul, MN 55164-0383
U.S.A.

FIRST EDITION
First Printing, 1993

International Standard Book Number: 0-87542-395-7

LLEWELLYN PUBLICATIONS
A Division of Llewellyn Worldwide, Ltd.
P.O. Box 64383, St. Paul, MN 55164-0383

NUMEROLOGY

Modern numerology assigns three numbers to a personal name: one for the vowels, one for the consonants, and one combining both. And in numerology a birth date is reduced to a single number. These four resultant numbers are then interpreted in light of the symbolic meanings for the numbers 1 through 9. This pamphlet will show you all you need to know about the modern methods of numerology, including simple step by step instructions for numbering your own name and birth date, as well as a wealth of divinatory interpretations for your personal numbers, from both modern and ancient sources.

DIVINATION

By stars, cards, and alphabets. These are the three most popular methods of divination that have survived into the 20th century. The three occult sciences governing these oracular techniques are astrology (divination by the placement of the stars), cartomancy (divination by the random fall of the tarot or playing cards), and numerology (divination by the numbers concealed in the letters of a name or the digits of a birth date).

This pamphlet will detail the third oracular method, known as numerology. The word "numerology" comes from the Latin *numeralis,* meaning figure, character, or number. The dictionary definition of modern numerology is, "the belief in the occult influence of numbers upon the life of an individual."[1]

Of the three methods of astrology, cartomancy, and numerology, numerology is the easiest oracular technique to learn and master. The term "numerology" appears to have become popular in the 19th-century literature of popular occultism. The source for this term in the European medieval magickal tradition is "arithmologia" (coined by Athanasius Kircher in 1665). Arithmologia is the combination of number *(arithmo)* and word *(logia).* It is the ancient divinatory[2] and meditational technique of giving number value to the letters of any word or name, and can be found in 13 distinct esoteric languages from ancient cuneiform to modern English.[3]

Gematria

Of all the ancient magickal languages, the mysticism surrounding biblical Hebrew is the best known in the West. The body of esoteric teachings concerning the Hebrew language is known as the Qabalah (meaning that knowledge which can only be imparted orally in secret, handed down from one generation to the next). In modern occultism, the term Qabalah, which originally meant Hebraic secret wisdom, has now come to mean any secret, esoteric system of thought which uses alphabet letter, color, symbol, sound, and number as the basic building blocks of its philosophical system. Thus modern writers will refer to a "Greek" Qabalah, a "Celtic" Qabalah, or even a "Wiccan" Qabalah.

The traditional Qabalistic science from which modern numerology has evolved is *gematria*. Gematria is the art of substituting a number value for any given word in Hebrew and finding a corresponding meaning in any other word equal to that specific number value. Gematria is a Rabbinical Hebrew term derived from Greek roots. It is a combination of *gramma* (letter) and *metria* (measure), to denote the measurement (or counting) of the letters composing any word, just as geometry is the measure *(metria)* of earth *(geo)*.[4]

MODERN NUMEROLOGY

Now modern numerology, having its antecedents in the Hebrew Qabalah, is a simplification of the very complicated number system charted out by the ancient rabbis. The main difference between modern numerology and ancient gematria is the scope of symbolic attributes for the number series. The ancient Hebrew Qabalah gave deep, rich metaphors for every whole integer in the number series as far as one can count. Thus the numbers 6, 60, and 600 each has its own unique poetical number metaphor, while in modern numerology 6, 60, and 600 are each interpreted as the single digit "6." For in modern numerology only the first nine numbers are symbolically significant, the number metaphors beyond nine having been lost to time.[5]

Pythagoras

Beyond the ancient Hebraic source for modern numerology, one other esoteric tradition for numbers should be mentioned: the Pythagorean school of numerical philosophy. As the Hebraic number code may have its source as far back as 1500 BCE, Pythagoras' famous school of number philosophers was founded in Crotona around 529 BCE. Most of what we know of the Pythagorean number doctrine comes from the historical writings of Diogenes Laertius (around the third century CE).

Basically, the Pythagorean doctrine views the number series as the basis from which God created the Universe. The first ten numbers are each given symbolic attributes, and ultimately any word in

Greek could be calculated as a number, thus connecting word to number. Any divine name of a Greek Goddess or God could be numbered, as well as any proper name. Thus, Pythagoras' own name by this ancient Greek numerological method was numbered as 864.[6]

By the ancient Pythagorean technique of numerology, a symbolic meaning would be given to the name Pythagoras by finding other words equal in number value to 864. But by modern numerology, to find the symbolic meaning of this name, the three digits composing the number 864 would be reduced, by addition, to a one digit number known as the digital root.

Let's try this modern method as an example. Pythagoras' number in Greek is 864. By adding the 3 digits composing this number we get $8 + 6 + 4 = 18$. Since 18 is beyond 9, we must do one more addition/reduction.[7] Thus 18 become $1 + 8 = 9$.

English Numerology

Modern numerology really came into vogue at the turn of the 19th century. Early attempts at making a Qabalah for English often paralleled the English alphabet to Hebrew and Greek. But the alphanumeric code for numerology that is most common today is based not on Hebrew or Greek roots, but rather the simple serial order of the English alphabet. This code is shown on the next page.

Numerologists, in analyzing your personal name with these number values, typically use three divinatory calculations, those of:

1. Motives—ideals or one's own deepest desires (Inner Life)

2. Appearances—one's personality, influence and impression on others (Outer Life)

3. Methods—one's true will, self-expression, conduct in the world (Path in Life)

These three calculations are obtained by adding together and reducing to one digit:

1. All the vowels of a name (Motives)

2. All the consonants of a name (Appearances)

3. Both the vowels and consonants of a name (Methods)[8]

3

These terms produce the following formula, where the sum of the number for Motives and the number for Appearances is always equal to the sum of all the letters in the name:

$$(MOTIVES) + (APPEARANCES) = (METHODS)$$

Modern Numerology

Alphabet Letter	Serial Order	Addition/ Reduction	Number Value
A	1	1	1
B	2	2	2
C	3	3	3
D	4	4	4
E	5	5	5
F	6	6	6
G	7	7	7
H	8	8	8
I	9	9	9
J	10	$1 + 0 = 1$	1
K	11	$1 + 1 = 2$	2
L	12	$1 + 2 = 3$	3
M	13	$1 + 3 = 4$	4
N	14	$1 + 4 = 5$	5
O	15	$1 + 5 = 6$	6
P	16	$1 + 6 = 7$	7
Q	17	$1 + 7 = 8$	8
R	18	$1 + 8 = 9$	9
S	19	$1 + 9 = 10/1 + 0 = 1$	1
T	20	$2 + 0 = 2$	2
U	21	$2 + 1 = 3$	3
V	22	$2 + 2 = 4$	4
W	23	$2 + 3 = 5$	5
X	24	$2 + 4 = 6$	6
Y	25	$2 + 5 = 7$	7
Z	26	$2 + 6 = 8$	8

By reducing the 26 letters of the English alphabet to the numbers 1 through 9 we get the following familiar numerological chart:

Number Grid for the English Alphabet

1	2	3	4	5	6	7	8	9
A	B	C	D	E	F	G	H	I
J	K	L	M	N	O	P	Q	R
S	T	U	V	W	X	Y	Z	

Example

As an example of the use of the formula of Motives, Appearances, and Methods, let's use the name of the founder of the Theosophical Society, Helena Petrovna Blavatsky, the most influential woman in the development of modern occultism. This name is made up of 8 vowels and 15 consonants. (Note: In modern numerology "Y" is always a consonant; the five vowels are A, E, I, O, U). The three basic calculations are as follows:

1. *Motives*—The eight vowels in the name Helena Petrovna Blavatsky are E, E, A, E, O, A, A, and A, which when added together equal $(E = 5) + (E = 5) + (A = 1) + (E = 5) + (O = 6) + (A = 1) + (A = 1) + (A = 1) = 25 = 2 + 5 = 7$.
Thus the number governing her ideals or deepest desires is **7**.

2. *Appearances*—The 15 consonants in Helena Petrovna Blavatsky are H, L, N, P, T, R, V, N, B, L, V, T, S, K, and Y, which when added together equal $(H = 8) + (L = 3) + (N = 5) + (P = 7) + (T = 2) + (R = 9) + (V = 4) + (N = 5) + (B = 2) + (L = 3) + (V = 4) + (T = 2) + (S = 1) + (K = 2) + (Y = 7) = 64 = 6 + 4 = 10 = 1 + 0 = 1$.
Thus the number governing her personality is **1**.

3. *Methods*—The 23 letters in Helena Petrovna Blavatsky combine 25 (the vowels) and 64 (the consonants), totaling to 89. 89 reduces to 17, which in turn reduces to 8 $(25 + 64 = 89 = 8 + 9 = 17 = 1 + 7 = 8)$.
Thus the number governing her conduct in the world is **8**.

Therefore by modern numerology the name Helena Petrovna Blavatsky is generated by the number series 7:1:8.

Birth Number

Numerology, in addition to assigning three basic number values to the letters of a name, also assigns a birth date to one number, known as the birth number. The birth number reveals influences at birth which will shape the direction your life will take. The birth date is first converted to three basic numbers, one for the month, one for the day, and one for the year. These three dates are then added together and reduced to a single number between 1 and 9.

Let's continue using Madame Blavatsky as our example and find her birth number. Helena Petrovna Blavatsky was born on August 11–12, 1831. (Born near midnight; the day to be used in our calculations can either 11 or 12.) The month, August, is the number 8 (January = 1, December = 12). The day, either 11 or 12, gives us $1 + 1 = 2$ or $1 + 2 = 3$. The year, 1831, reduces to $1 + 8 + 3 + 1 = 13 = 1 + 3 = 4$. Therefore the birth number of Madame Blavatsky is either $8 + 2 + 4 = 14 = 1 + 4 = 5$ (using August 11) or $8 + 3 + 4 = 15 = 1 + 5 = 6$ (using August 12), either the number 5 or the number 6.[9]

THE MEANINGS OF THE NUMBERS

But what good is this bit of divinatory calculation associating numbers to names and birth dates if we do not have an oracular vocabulary which can give symbolic meaning and nuance to the number series? Luckily, modern numerology has inherited from the ancient tradition of numbers a key to interpreting the meaning of numbers.

As pointed out above, modern numerology only possesses a divinatory tradition for the first nine numbers. Each of these nine numbers has its own unique divinatory significance. The following table gives the typical symbolic correspondences for these numbers.

The Nine Numbers of Modern Numerology

NUMBER	DIVINATORY MEANING
1	Initiative, independence, forcefulness (masculine number)
2	Diplomacy, tact, attention to detail (feminine number)
3	Spiritual, ambition, self-expression, easy success, lucky
4	Material, labor, routine work with little monetary compensation, unlucky
5	Imagination, inventive genius, charm, restlessness, adventurous

6	Tenacity, conscientiousness, success by working with another, domestic
7	Mysticism, magick, occultism, isolation, poets and dreamers; to be misunderstood by one's associates
8	Judgment, reason, organization, financial success
9	Sympathy, generosity; dramatic, artistic talent (higher octave—teacher, master)

These nine basic meanings have a pattern to their symbolism. The first eight numbers form four pairs of contrasts, while the ninth number sums up and balances these four opposite couplings. The odd numbers 1, 3, 5, and 7 are celestial in nature, while the even numbers 2, 4, 6, and 8 are terrestrial. The number 9 counterbalances the four spiritual odd and the four earthly even numbers. The following table shows this key to the nine numbers.

Key to the Nine Numbers of Modern Numerology

CELESTIAL ODD	TERRESTRIAL EVEN
1 (Active)	2 (Receptive)
3 (Spiritual)	4 (Earthly)
5 (Imaginative)	6 (Practical)
7 (Success in spiritual matters)	8 (Success in material endeavors)

A synthesis of first 8 numbers:

9

(a harmony between spiritual and material pursuits)

Two other numbers beyond 1 through 9 in modern numerology are regarded as special or gifted numbers. These numbers are 11 and 22. Eleven is the number of revelation, while 22 is the number of adeptship. Whenever the number 11 or 22 is generated, either by totaling numbers together or reducing and then adding together the digits of a number, then the special meanings apply for 11 and 22 rather than the reduced 2 or 4.

The number 11 symbolizes inner vision that contains a message that must be communicated to the world in the form of an inspired text, a religious or philosophical doctrine, or a new teaching. The number 22 symbolizes the master, either good or evil, white or black magick. Note that 11 can degenerate to 2 (1 + 1) and 22 can degenerate to 4 (2 + 2). Thus divine revelation (11) can turn to mere receptivity to any influence (good or evil), while adeptship (22) can turn to depression or grim, hard work (4).[10]

Beyond the exoteric divinatory interpretations of numerology, pioneer occultists have been able to give the spiritual, or esoteric, nature of the first nine numbers. Madame Blavatsky, in her *Secret Doctrine*, gives the mystery-language symbols for the first nine numbers. Aleister Crowley and Paul Foster Case have given a Qabalistic-tarot oriented interpretation of the symbolic use of numbers. Sepharial and Isidore Kozminsky offer in their writings variations on the meanings modern numerology assigns to the numbers 1 through 9.[11] The table on the next page gives these additional systems of interpretation for modern numerology.

The source for all these diverse meanings for the number series of modern numerology is the ancient number lore of the Chinese, Hellenistic and Semitic esoteric traditions. Chinese Taoism allocated a lucky or unlucky quality to the first nine numbers. The Pythagoreans gave us philosophical titles to interpret these same nine numbers, while the Hebrew rabbinical mystics described the Tree of Life as a set of mystical titles for the number series.

Chinese Taoism classifies the entire universe in terms of yang and yin, odd and even numbers. The first nine numbers are drawn upon a magick square of nine cells (the Western source for the square of Saturn):

Square of 9 as Good and Bad Luck

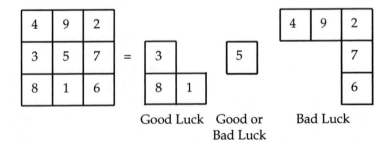

Modern Esoteric Interpretations of the Numbers 1 Through 9

NUMBER	BLAVATSKY	CROWLEY	CASE	SEPHARIAL	KOZMINSKY
1	A living, standing being, divine, celestial	The point, spirit	Beginning, initiative, unity	Manifestation, assertion positive, active	Ambition, intention, passion
2	Imperfect state, fall, branching, terrestrial, devilish, unlucky	The point distinguishable from one other, change	Dualism, reflection receptivity	Antithesis, witness, confirmation, dualism	Death, destruction, fatality
3	Mystery, spiritual man, triangle	The point defined by relation to two others, fertilized idea	Multiplication, development, growth	Volition, procedure, penetration	Destiny, faith, soul, religion
4	Immortality, Physical, matter, animal	Matter, solidification	Order, measurement, classification	Reality, expansion, experience, classification	Strength, power, wisdom, solidity
5	Disorder, confusion, universe, the five limbs of man	Motion(time), storm and stress	Mediation, adaption, activity	Expansion, comprehensive, judgment, increase	Marriage pleasure, happiness, the stars
6	Earth asleep during autumn, winter; the world ready to be animated by spirit	Self-conscious, center	Balance, harmony	Cooperation, marriage, communion, sympathy	Perfected labor
7	Earth awake during spring, summer; life eternal; man as spiritual and physical	Bliss degeneration	Rest, safety, security	Completion, duration, stability, perfection	Ideal happiness, freedom, rest, way of life
8	Eternal, spiral motion of cycles	Thought, correction of previous error	Rhythm, vibration, alternate cycles	Dissolution, revolution, separation, inspiration	Protection, justice
9	Incessant reproduction, multiplication	Being, crystallization of energy	Completion, attainment, realization	Regeneration, spirituality, dreaming, mystery	Anxiety, imperfection, grief

These nine numbers in turn were connected to the divinatory symbols used in the I Ching, the oldest surviving oracular textbook. The oracular nature for these first nine numbers was then determined by the relationship between the numbers, their direction on the square of nine cells, and their parallel to the eight trigrams which make up the 64 hexagrams of the I Ching. The table below shows the lucky or unlucky nature of the first nine numbers.[12]

The Pythagoreans gave us philosophical titles to interpret these same nine numbers. In the Pythagorean school of thought the first ten numbers, known as the Decad, were given a host of symbolic images. The below table shows the main philosophical attributes given to the first nine numbers by the Pythagoreans.[13]

The Hebrew rabbinical mystics, known as the Qabalists, viewed the universe as a set of interlocking wheels or emanations, which fall to ten basic divisions. These ten divisions are the first ten numbers, forming the framework of the Tree of Life which spans the infinite universe. The below table shows the primary titles for the first nine numbers of the Tree of Life.[14]

The Numbers 1 Through 9 According to Ancient Number Lore

NUMBER	CHINESE NUMBER ORACLES	PYTHAGOREAN NUMBER PHILOSOPHY	QABALISTIC NUMBERS
1	Lucky	Unity	Crown
2	Error	Indefinite	Wisdom
3	Good Luck	Harmony	Understanding
4	Regret	Permanency (The Square)	Mercy
5	A balance between good and bad luck	Equilibrium	Severity
6	Rejection	Marriage	Beauty
7	Catastrophe	Victory	Victory
8	Fortune	Love	Splendor
9	Bad Luck	Concord	Foundation

From this ancient numerical symbolism an astrological character can be established for the numbers 1 through 9. Both the Eastern Chinese and Western Semitic-Hellenistic zodiacs can be correlated to these numbers. The following chart gives these astrological correspondences.[15]

The Chinese and Hebraic Astrological Correspondences
for the Numbers 1 Through 9

| | ——— CHINESE TAOISM ——— | | ——— HEBREW QABALISM ——— | |
NUMBER	PLANET	SIGN	PLANET	SIGN
1	Mercury	Monkey, Cock, Pig, Dog	The impulse beyond all planetary and zodiacal influences	
2	Saturn	Snake	The zodiac of 12 signs	
3	Jupiter	Rat	Saturn	Capricorn and Aquarius
4	Jupiter	Ox	Jupiter	Sagittarius and Pisces
5	Earth as center of Universe	Sun as center of zodiacal belt	Mars	Aries and Scorpio
6	Venus	Horse	Sun	Leo
7	Venus	Sheep	Venus	Taurus and Libra
8	Saturn	Dragon	Mercury	Gemini and Virgo
9	Mars	Tiger, Rabbit	Moon	Cancer

One last ancient system of numerical symbolism should be shown here, and that is the tarot.[16] The first 22 pictorial cards of the tarot each bear a Hebrew letter and a number. The nine cards which are numbered 1 through 9 (usually in Roman numerals) represent in picture form the Western esoteric interpretation of the number series. The table on the following page gives the barest meanings for these symbols.

Tarot Interpretations of the Numbers 1 Through 9

NUMBER	TAROT CARD	SYMBOLIC MEANING OF NUMBER
1	I—The Magician	Concentration, intention, will
2	II—The High Priestess	Reflection, receptivity, hidden knowledge
3	III—The Empress	Imagination, inspiration, spiritual world
4	IV—The Emperor	Reason, order, material world
5	V—The Hierophant	Intuition, union, bridging of spiritual and material (Heaven and Earth)
6	VI—The Lovers	Decision, discrimination, love
7	VII—The Chariot	Direction, empowerment, secret languages (symbolic)
8	VIII—Strength	Energy, exuberance, bliss
9	IX—The Hermit	Summit, attainment, secret teachers

Now, finally, using the basic interpretations for the numbers 1 through 9, and the four numbers we derived from the divinatory calculations shown in previous examples, we can numerically analyze Helena Petrovna Blavatsky's name and her birth date.

Name: HELENA PETROVNA BLAVATSKY

1. Blavatsky's "Motives" are governed by the number 7. Using the divinatory meaning for this number we find that "Mysticism" describes her ideals and deepest desires. This is a very good description of the deep spiritual drive that operated throughout her life.

2. Blavatsky's "Appearance" is governed by the number 1. The divinatory meaning for the number 1 reveals an "Independent and Forceful" personality and appearance (1 being a masculine number). Blavatsky's appearance and bearing have been referred to as both masculine and forceful by many of her biographers. The number 1 presents a very accurate picture of Madame Blavatsky.

3. Blavatsky's "Methods" are governed by the number 8. The divinatory meaning for the number 8 describes a life path of "Finan-

cial Success and Organization." Blavatsky's ability to co-found the Theosophical Society, and make it financially solvent, can easily be described by this correspondence.

Birth date: July 30/31, 1831
Blavatsky has two birth numbers, 5 and 6. It seems when looking at her life that the "Restless, Imaginative and Adventurous Spirit" associated to the number 5, rather than the "Sedate, Domestic" spirit associated to the number 6, dominated her life. However, in addition to her restless and adventurous nature, she was a tenacious woman able to achieve success by working with others (qualities of the number 6).

Our numerical analysis reveals a mystic with an independent and forceful nature who seeks financial success through organization, a restless, tenacious, and adventurous spirit with an ability to work with others to achieve success. Our analysis reveals Helena Petrovna Blavatsky.

The following rules summarize the basics of modern numerology.

Rules for Calculating and Interpreting the Key Numbers Used in Numerological Analysis: The Three Numbers Associated to Name and the Birth Number

A. Name (Three Numbers)
  1. Motive (Ideals)
     (a) Write down all the vowels in the name.
     (b) Convert each vowel to its corresponding number
         (A = 1, U = 3, E = 5, O = 6, I = 9).
     (c) Add these numbers together.
     (d) Reduce this total to a one-digit number (1–9) by repeatedly adding the digits of the number together until a one-digit number is obtained.
     (e) Find the key phrase corresponding to the resultant number to discover the Ideals or Motives (see below, Key Words).
  2. Appearance (Personality)
     (a) Write down all the consonants in the name.
     (b) Convert each consonant to its corresponding number
         (J, S = 1; B, K, T = 2; C, L = 3; D, M, V = 4; N, W = 5; F, X = 6; G, P, Y = 7; H, Q, Z = 8; R = 9).
     (c) Add these numbers together.
     (d) Reduce this total to a one-digit number (1–9) by repeatedly adding the digits of the number together until a one-digit number is obtained.

(e) Find the key phrase corresponding to the resultant number to discover the Personality or Appearance (see below, Key Words).

3. Methods (Life Path)

(a) Add together the number values obtained above for the vowels and the consonants.

(b) Reduce this total to a one-digit number (1–9) by repeatedly adding the digits of the number together until a one-digit number is obtained.

(c) Find the key phrase corresponding to the resultant number to discover the Life Path or Methods (see below, Key Words).

B. Birth Number

(a) Write out the date of birth as digits of a number.

Month—Use the numbers 1 through 12 to designate January through December.

Day—Use the numbers 1 through 31 for the days of the month.

Year—Use the century as well as year to designate birth year (use 1993 instead of 93).

(b) Add together the digits of the number obtained in (a).

(c) Reduce this total to a one-digit number (1–9) by repeatedly adding the digits of the number together until a one-digit number is obtained.

(d) Find the key phrase corresponding to the resultant number to discover the influence one inherits at birth (see below Key Words).[17]

C. Key Words for the Numbers 1 Through 9

1 Independent
2 Receptive
3 Spiritual
4 Material
5 Imaginative
6 Practical
7 Mystical
8 Wealthy
9 Generous (higher octave: Teacher)

Finally, there are other systems for numbering the English alphabet that have been popular in the last 100 years of modern numerology. Five alternate number values are shown in the following table.

Alternate Number Values for Modern Numerology

ALPHABET	HEBREW VALUE	FADIC CODE	CROWLEY HEBREW	GREEK VALUE	GERMAN ROSICRUCIAN
A	1	1	1, 10, 70	1	1
B	2	2	2, 6	2	2
C	3	3	3, 20, 100	3	3
D	4	4	4	4	4
E	5	5	1, 5, 10	5	5
F	80	8	6, 80	6	6
G	3	3	3	7	7
H	5	5	5, 8	8	8
I	10	1	1, 10, 6	9	9
J	10	1	10	10	10
K	20	2	8, 20, 100	20	11
L	30	3	30	30	12
M	40	4	40	40	13
N	50	5	50	50	14
O	70	7	1, 6, 10, 70	60	15
P	80	8	6, 80	70	16
Q	100	1	20, 100	80	17
R	200	2	200	90	18
S	300	3	7, 60, 90, 300	100	19
T	400	4	9, 400	200	20
U	6	6	6, 70	300	21
V	6	6	6, 80	400	22
W	6	6	6	500	23
X	500	5	60, 400	600	24
Y	10	1	10	700	25
Z	7	7	7, 60, 90	800	26

1. Hebrew Value

A very popular method of numbering English is the paralleling of the English alphabet phonetically to the Hebrew alphabet. These numbers result in very high values for names in English. However, the method for calculation is the same, that of reducing the final number total to a single digit.

As an example let's number the name of the leading 20th-century exponent on the Qabalistic tarot, Paul Foster Case. Using Hebrew number values, the following numbers are obtained:

Name: PAUL FOSTER CASE =
    (80 + 1 + 6 + 30) + (80 + 70 + 300 + 400 + 5 + 200) +
        (3 + 1 + 300 + 5)
    1. Motives (the vowels) =
        (1 + 6) + (70 + 5) + (1 + 5) = 88 = 16 = 7
    2. Appearances (the consonants) =
        (80 + 30) + (80 + 300 + 400 + 200) + (3 + 300) = 1393 = 16 = 7
    3. Methods (all letters) =
        (117) + (1055) + (309) = 1481 = 14 = 5

This is a good example where the inner and outer roles played out in life are one and the same. By this analysis, Case's Inner Life and Outer Life are each governed by "7," mysticism and magick, and his Path in Life by "5," inventive genius and exploration.

2. Fadic Code

This popular English-Hebrew code takes the values from the preceding Hebrew code and removes all zeros in the number values (the same digital root numbers generated by the Hebrew value will be obtained using this Fadic Code). This code has been shown in the writings of Manly P. Hall (although it was not invented by Hall).

As an example of the Fadic Code let's number the name of the leading founder of the Order of The Golden Dawn, Samuel Liddell MacGregor Mathers.

Name: SAMUEL LIDDELL MACGREGOR MATHERS =
    (3 + 1 + 4 + 6 + 5 + 3) + (3 + 1 + 4 + 4 + 5 + 3 + 3) +
        (4 + 1 + 3 + 3 + 2 + 5 + 3 + 7 + 2) + (4 + 1 + 4 + 5 + 5 + 2 + 3)
    1. Motives (the vowels) =
        (1 + 6 + 5) + (1 + 5) + (1 + 5 + 7) + (1 + 5) = 37 = 10 = 1
    2. Appearances (the consonants) =
        (3 + 4 + 3) + (3 + 4 + 4 + 3 + 3) + (4 + 3 + 3 + 2 + 3 + 2) +
            (4 + 4 + 5 + 2 + 3) = 62 = 8
    3. Methods (all letters) =
        (22) + (23) + (30) + (24) = 99 = 18 = 9

By this analysis Mathers' Inner Life is governed by "1," independent and original thinking; his Outer Life by "8," organizational skills; while his Life Path is governed by "9," in this case the path of a teacher.

Mathers' complete name numbers to 99, which reduces to 9. The "9" is overtly emphasized, symbolizing the highest octave of 9, which is the teacher or master as portrayed in the tarot as Key 9, The Hermit.

Note that this mystical value of 99 is only possible when the name "MacGregor" is worked into the calculation. Mathers added this name to his own personal name for magickal and mystical purposes.

3. Crowley's Hebrew-English

Throughout his lifetime, Aleister Crowley turned English magickal and mystical terms to Hebrew and then to number. He used many variant values for each English letter, and he often represented two or more English alphabet letters as one Hebrew letter. However, he seldom reduced a high number to a single digit, but rather he interpreted that high number by paralleling it to another word or phrase of equal numerical value.

During his magickal career, Crowley identified with the apocalyptic number 666. By ingenious use of his own phonetic Hebrew-English Qabalah, he was able to number his name as 666 in two ways.[18]

1. Aleister Crowley as ALISTIR QRVLI (אליסטיר קרולי) =
   (1 + 30 + 10 + 60 + 9 + 10 + 200) + (100 + 200 + 6 + 30 + 10) = 666
   (here the English EI, E, and EY are each valued as the Hebrew I)

2. Aleister E. Crowley as ALHISTHR H KROVLHI
   (אליסטהר ה כרעולהי) =
   (1 + 30 + 5 + 10 + 60 + 9 + 5 + 200) + (5) + (20 + 200 + 70 + 6 + 30 + 5 + 10) = 666 (here each English letter is given a Hebrew equivalent)

Note that as a Methods or Life Path number, 666 reduces to 9, the number of teacher and master.

4. Greek Value

Another popular method of numbering English is to parallel the 26 letters of the English alphabet to the range of numbers 1 through 800 (corresponding to the Greek letters of alpha and omega). Surprisingly, when all zeroes are removed from these "Greek" numbers, they parallel exactly those values of traditional modern numerology. For example, Z, which is 800 in the Greek code, is 8 by modern numerology. Unlike the Hebrew code, this parallel between Greek and English is not phonetic.

As an example, let's number the name Arthur Edward Waite, creator of the most popular tarot deck of all times. More copies of the Waite tarot deck exist than any other tarot deck ever printed.

Name: ARTHUR EDWARD WAITE =
  (1 + 90 + 200 + 8 + 300 + 90) + (5 + 4 + 500 + 1 + 90 + 4) +
  (500 + 1 + 9 + 200 + 5)
  1. Motives (the vowels) =
     (1 + 300) + (5 + 1) + (1 + 9 + 5) = 322 = 7
  2. Appearances (the consonants) =
     (90 + 200 + 8 + 90) + (4 + 500 + 90 + 4) + (500 + 200) = 1686 = 21
     = 3
  3. Methods (all letters) =
     (689) + (604) + (715) = 2008 = 10 = 1

By this analysis, Waite's Inner Life is governed by "7," mysticism; his Outer Life by "3," spiritual matters; and his Path in Life by "1," originality and inventive genius.

5. German Rosicrucian Serial Order

This traditional serial order value for English can be used when a higher number value than 9 is needed for any given name or word. This code was extensively used in Rosicrucian and Alchemical writings and had its origin in the 26-lettered German alphabet. It is directly referred to in the Rosicrucian text, *The Chymical Wedding of Christian Rosenkreutz* (1616) written by Johann Valentin Andreae. Christian Rosenkreutz is the mythical founder of the Rosicrucian Movement (born 1378 CE).

As an example let's number this mythical name using the German Rosicrucian Serial Order code.

Name: CHRISTIAN ROSENKREUTZ =
  (3 + 8 + 18 + 9 + 19 + 20 + 9 + 1 + 14) +
  (18 + 15 + 19 + 5 + 14 + 11 + 18 + 5 + 21 + 20 + 26)
  1. Motives (the vowels) =
     (9 + 9 + 1) + (15 + 5 + 5 + 21) = 65 = 11 = 2
  2. Appearances (the consonants) =
     (3 + 8 + 18 + 19 + 20 + 14) + (18 + 19 + 14 + 11 + 18 + 20 + 26)
     = 208 = 10 = 1
  3. Methods (all letters) =
     (101) + (172) = 273 = 12 = 3

By this analysis, Christian Rosenkreutz's Inner Life is governed by "2," receptivity; his Outer Life by "1," initiation; and his Path in Life is governed by "3," spiritual work. Outwardly he initiated (1) a new spiritual movement (3) which he had received internally (2) from higher sources.

The Method of Habih Ahmad

There is one last variation of modern numerology which has almost been lost to time that should be shown now. In 1903 Habih Ahmad developed a set of number values for the English alphabet based on their phonetic equivalence in Hebrew.[19] This code resembles the phonetic Qabalah based on Hebrew developed by Crowley. Like Crowley, Ahmad allowed certain combined consonants to stand for one number. For instance, if the letters SH appear in a name, they are seen as one letter and numbered like the phonetic Hebrew equivalent, Sh (Shin), as 3(00). Unique to Ahmad's system is the rule for double letters. If any successive two letters of a name are the same consonant (or vowel), they are numbered as if they were one letter. For example, the word GODDESS would be numbered using the letters GODES. Austin Spare developed a similar technique in designing his own magickal sigils using the English alphabet.

The table on the next page gives the essential attributes of Ahmad's system. The astrological symbolism for the nine numbers, as well as the symbolic meanings given are unique to Ahmad's research.

As an example of Ahmad's code for English, let's number the name William Wynn Westcott, one of the three founders of the occult order, The Golden Dawn.

Name: WILLIAM WYNN WESTCOTT =
   (6 + 1 + 3 + 1 + 1 + 4) + (6 + 1 + 5) + (6 + 1 + 8 + 4 + 2 + 6 + 4)
   1. Motives (the vowels) =
      (1 + 1 + 1) + (1) + (1 + 6) = 11
      (Note: "y" is a vowel in Ahmad's system, valued at 1)
   2. Appearances (the consonants) =
      (6 + 3 + 4) + (6 + 5) + (6 + 8 + 4 + 2 + 4) = 48 = 12 = 3
      (Note: LL = 3, NN = 5, TT = 4, all examples of double letters
      counted as one letter)
   3. Methods (all letters) =
      (16) + (12) + (31) = 59 = 14 = 5

By this analysis, William Wynn Westcott's Inner Life is governed by 11, a spiritual revelation to share with the world; his Outer Life by 3, spiritual matters; and his Path in Life by 5, adventurous explorations into the unknown. (Note also that by Ahmad's code Westcott's initials of W.W.W. equal 666.)

19

Ahmad's Sound and Number Correlation for the English Alphabet

NUMBER	HEBREW MODEL	ENGLISH ALPHABET	PLANET	ZODIAC	ASTROLOGICAL MEANING	PHONETIC MEANING	NUMBER MEANING
1	A, I, Q	A, E, I, Y	Sun (+)	Leo	Light	Calm	Spiritual Balance
2	B, K, R	B, K, Q, R C (hard)	Moon (-)	Cancer	Receptivity	Between Heavy and Hard	Worldly Affairs
3	G, L, Sh	G, J, L, Ch, Sh	Jupiter	Sagittarius Pisces	Justice	Sweet	Refining Worldly
4	D, M, Th	D, M, T	Sun (-)	Leo Gemini	Heat	Pure	Balance
5	H, N	H, N	Mercury	Virgo Taurus	Intelligence	Distinct	Mental Activity
6	V, S	W, O, U	Venus	Libra	Balance	Rich	Comfort
7	O, Z	Z, S(hard), X	Moon (+)	Cancer	Transmitting	Between Heavy and Hard	Link Between Spirit and Matter
8	Ch, P	S, C(soft) Ch (Guttural) P, F, Ph, V	Saturn	Capricorn Aquarius	Purifying	Sad	Physical Cessation
9	T, Tz	Th, Ts	Mars	Aries Scorpio	Warlike	Rough	Force

As shown throughout this pamphlet, the simple rules of modern numerology evolved from a much more complex science of symbolism, allocating number values to words. At least 13 distinct traditions have developed in the last 5,000 years to impart a special symbolic meaning to each and every number. These traditions are completely deciphered and reconstructed in my book, *The Key of It All*. This *Truth About* pamphlet gives a tantalizing glimpse into the power and range of this ancient number-language tradition.

NOTES

1. *New Webster's Dictionary*, 1981, p. 651.

2. Divination by numbers alone is also referred to as *arithmomancy*. This system gives concrete meanings to any given number, which serves as the oracular message when that particular number is encountered in divination, dreams, or visions.

3. See *The Key of It All*, forthcoming from Llewellyn, for a complete analysis of these 13 esoteric number-language traditions.

4. The original Hebrew Qabalah used in gematria is as follows.

Hebrew Qabalah Used in Gematria

HEBREW LETTER	ENGLISH	NUMBER VALUE	HEBREW LETTER	ENGLISH	NUMBER VALUE
א	A	1	ל	L	30
ב	B	2	מ	M	40
ג	G	3	נ	N	50
ד	D	4	ס	S	60
ה	H	5	ע	O	70
ו	V	6	פ	P	80
ז	Z	7	צ	Tz	90
ח	Ch	8	ק	Q	100
ט	T	9	ר	R	200
י	I	10	ש	Sh	300
כ	K	20	ת	Th	400

5. In this sense modern numerology is a degeneration of a much more complex system which gives symbolic meanings to every number in the infinite number series. But as I show later in this pamphlet, modern numerology has preserved, in part, the true symbolic meanings for the first nine numbers, as established by the mystery schools of ancient China, Greece, and Israel.

6. The name Pythagoras in Greek is Πυθαγορας (PUThAGORAS). As numbers, the letters of the name become 80 + 400 + 9 + 1 + 3 + 70 + 100 + 1 + 200, which totals to 864. Therefore, Pythagoras' name would conceal the number 864. The original Greek Qabalah is given here.

The Greek Qabalah

GREEK LETTER	ENGLISH	NUMBER VALUE	GREEK LETTER	ENGLISH	NUMBER VALUE
A, α	A	1	N, ν	N	50
B, β	B	2	Ξ, ξ	X	60
Γ, γ	G	3	O, o	O	70
Δ, δ	D	4	Π, π	P	80
E, ε	E	5	P, ρ	R	100
Z, ζ	Z	7	Σ, σ, ς	S	200
H, η	H	8	T, τ	T	300
Θ, θ	Th	9	Υ, υ	U	400
I, ι	I	10	Φ. φ	Ph	500
K, κ	K	20	X, χ	Ch	600
Λ, λ	L	30	Ψ, ψ	Ps	700
M, μ	M	40	Ω, ω	Ō	800

7. In the late 19th- and early 20th-century occult literature, this method is known as "Theosophical Reduction." It appears in the Qabalistic writings of Paul Foster Case, among others. I can find no source in Blavatsky's copious writings for this name or method, but I believe it may have come out of the Theosophical work of Wynn Westcott (one of the original three secret chiefs of The Golden Dawn). Westcott, among other things, was Blavatsky's advisor for all Hermetic and Qabalistic entries in her *Theosophical Glossary* (1892).

8. I derive these techniques from an obscure occult pamphlet from the 1920s called *Numerology* by Malcolm Madison. Other techniques may vary in title or name, but the method described here is the essential 20th century treatment of name analysis.

Two other techniques in some systems of modern numerology are not detailed in this pamphlet: reducing to a single digit either the total number of letters composing a name, or the number values of the initials of a name.

9. The traditional Theosophical dating for Blavatsky's birth can be found on page xxvi or her *Collected Writings* (vol. I). The exact date of birth was 11:22 PM (Greenwich time), July 30, 1831, by the Julian (Old Style) calendar, and August 11, 1831, by the Gregorian (current) calendar. Either date reduces to the number 5:

$$7/30/1831 = 7 + 3 + 0 + 1 + 8 + 3 + 1 = 23 = 5$$
$$8/11/1831 = 8 + 1 + 1 + 1 + 8 + 3 + 1 = 23 = 5$$

10. The use of 11 and 22 as the only numbers beyond 9 with any meaning betrays a Hebraic influence, or source, for the word metaphors given to the first nine numbers in modern numerology. For 22 is one of the key numbers in the Hebrew Qabalah, the Hebrew alphabet being composed of 22 letters. And half of 22 is 11, the middle, or center, of the Hebrew alphabet. Two other apparent occult systems show this Qabalistic influence of 22: (1) the 22 chapters of the Revelation, the last book of the New Testament, and (2) the 22 pictorial keys of the Major Arcana in the tarot. Basically, by the word metaphors concealed in the ancient magickal languages, 11 symbolizes solitary study of the universe without the aid of a teacher, while 22 symbolizes both a great cycle coming to a conclusion and secret knowledge possessed by the esoteric teachers of the world.

11. The sources used for these modern interpretations of the nine basic numbers are:

1. Blavatsky—H. P. Blavatsky, *The Secret Doctrine*, 1888, vol. 2, ch. 24, "The Cross and the Pythagorean Decade."
2. Crowley—A. E. Crowley, *777*, 1909, "Naples Arrangement" (p. 39); A.E. Crowley, *Book of Thoth*, 1944, pt. 4, "The Small Cards."
3. Case—P. F. Case, A Brief Analysis of the Tarot, 1927, "Occult Meaning of Numbers" (pp. 4–10).
4. Sepharial—Sepharial, *The Kabala of Numbers*, ch. 1, "The Power of Numbers."
5. Kozminsky—Isidore Kozminsky, *Numbers: Their Meaning and Magic*, 1912, "Symbols and Meanings of the Numbers" (pp. 6–30).

12. Refer to the 6th key of *The Key of It All* for a complete detailing of the Chinese Taoist number system, including a symbolic analysis of the I Ching.

13. Refer to the 7th key of *The Key of It All* for the complete set of symbolic attributes given to the Decad.

14. Refer to the 2nd key of *The Key of It All* for 149 tables of symbolic attributes for these first ten numbers (or sephiroth) on the Tree of Life.

15. The Chinese astrological attributes are generated by connecting the five Chinese elements to the five planets, and then to the 12 zodiacal year signs they rule. The Hebrew astrological attributes are

generated by connecting the planets which govern the first ten sephiroth with the zodiacal signs they rule.

16. Refer to the 12th key of *The Key of It All* for a complete detailing of the esoteric tradition concerning the tarot. The tarot is the original playing card deck introduced into Medieval Europe in the 14th century, as a pictorial key to the Hebrew Qabalah and the Greek Pythagorean doctrine of numbers.

17. Auspicious Day Calculation—In addition to the birth date calculation, there are two basic methods to determine if any given day is lucky or unlucky. The first method is based on modern numerology while the second is derived from the Chinese magick square of nine numbers.
    A. Harmonious Birth Date
        1. Reduce any day in question to a single-digit number, using the method for finding the birth number.
        2. If the resultant number is equal to your own birth number, it is a very powerful and lucky day for you. But the further away from your own number, the weaker that day becomes. Further, if the number is odd and your birth number is odd, there is harmony; but if one number is odd and the other even, there is strife.
    B. Chinese Auspicious Day
        1. Reduce any date in question to a single digit, using the same method as above.
        2. Whether the day in question is lucky or unlucky will depend on the following table.

Chinese Lucky Date Chart

Lucky Dates Reduce To	Unlucky Dates Reduce To
1	2
3	4
5	6
8	7
	9

18. From Crowley's *Equinox*, vol. I., no. 8 (1913), *Sepher Sephiroth*, p. 57. Note that the mystical number 666 is the only direct, overt example of the use of alphabet letters as number in both the Old and New Testaments of the Bible. This number appears in Revelation 13:18, in the form of a question asking the reader to calculate the number of

the beast. It is the number value of the "Beast" in Greek, for the Greek phrase, "The Great, Wild Beast" numbers to 666 in the original Greek code:

Name: The Great, Wild Beast
Greek: το μεγα θηριον (TO MEGA ThHRION)
Number: (300 + 70) + (40 + 5 + 3 + 1) + (9 + 8 + 100 + 10 + 70 + 50) = 666

It should be noted that Aleister Crowley's birth name was Edward Alexander Crowley. By modern numerology, this name generates 11:4:6, the inner personality of an adept (11), the outer personality (4) perceived by others as material and crass, and a life path of hard work requiring the aid of others (6). The three numbers, 11, 4, and 6, are also pre-eminent numbers in Crowley's own Qabalistic workings:

11 is a key number in his *Book of the Law.*

4 as 444 is one value of Crowley's most famous magickal axiom, "Do what thou wilt shall be the whole of the Law," by the number values of the German Rosicrucian English Qabalah (the serial order of the English alphabet).

6 as 666 is the "mark of the beast" in the Revelation (as shown above).

19. I derive this information from two works by Ahmad's wife Mabel:

1. Mabel L. Ahmad, *Names & Their Numbers,* 1925
2. Mabel L. Ahmad, *Sound and Number: The Law of Destiny and Design,* 1925

STAY IN TOUCH

On the following pages you will find some of the books now available on related subjects. Your book dealer stocks most of these and will stock new titles in the Llewellyn series as they become available. We urge your patronage.

To obtain our full catalog, to keep informed about new titles as they are released and to benefit from informative articles and helpful news, you are invited to write for our bimonthly news magazine/catalog, *Llewellyn's New Worlds of Mind and Spirit*. A sample copy is free, and it will continue coming to you at no cost as long as you are an active mail customer. Or you may subscribe for just $10.00 in the U.S.A. and Canada ($20.00 overseas, first class mail). Many bookstores also have *New Worlds* available to their customers. Ask for it.

Llewellyn's New Worlds of Mind and Spirit
P.O. Box 64383-395, St. Paul, MN 55164-0383, U.S.A.

* * *

TO ORDER BOOKS AND TAPES

If your book dealer does not have the books described, you may order them directly from the publisher by sending full price in U.S. funds, plus $3.00 for postage and handling for orders *under* $10.00; $4.00 for orders *over* $10.00. There are no postage and handling charges for orders over $50.00. Postage and handling rates are subject to change. We ship UPS whenever possible. Delivery guaranteed. Provide your street address as UPS does not deliver to P.O. Boxes. UPS to Canada requires a $50.00 minimum order. Allow 4-6 weeks for delivery. Orders outside the U.S.A. and Canada: Airmail—add retail price of book; add $5.00 for each non-book item (tapes, etc.); add $1.00 per item for surface mail. Credit card (VISA, MasterCard, American Express) orders are accepted. Charge card orders only ($15.00 minimum order) may be phoned in free within the U.S.A. or Canada by dialing 1-800-THE-MOON. For customer service, call 1-612-291-1970. Mail orders to:

LLEWELLYN PUBLICATIONS
P.O. Box 64383-395, St. Paul, MN 55164-0383, U.S.A.

THE KEY OF IT ALL
An Encyclopedic Guide to the Sacred Languages & Magical Systems of the World
by David Allen Hulse

This book is divided into 13 keys, or chapters, each completely deciphering and reconstructing one aspect of the great ancient tradition of number-language symbolism. Each chapter is a key unlocking one ancient magickal language.

Key 1. Cuneiform—The oldest tradition ascribing number to word; the symbolism of base 60 used in Babylonian and Sumerian Cuneiform; the first God and Goddess names associated to number.

Key 2. Hebrew—A complete exposition of the rules governing the Hebrew Qabalah; the evolution of the Tree of Life; an analysis of the Book of Formation, the oldest key to the symbolic meaning of the Hebrew alphabet.

Key 3. Arabic—The similarity between the Hebrew and Arabic Qabalahs; the secret Quranic symbolism for the Arabic alphabet; the Persian alphabet code; the philosophical numbering system of G. I. Gurdjieff.

Key 4. Sanskrit—The secret Vedic number codes for Sanskrit; the digital word-numbers; the symbolism of the seven chakras and their numerical key.

Key 5. Tibetan—The secret number lore for Tibetan as inspired by the Sanskrit codes; the secret symbols for the Tibetan alphabet; the six major schools of Tattva philosophy.

Key 6. Chinese—The Taoist calligraphic stroke count technique for number Chinese characters; Chinese Taoist number philosophy; the I Ching; the Japanese language and its parallels to the Chinese number system.

Key 7. Greek—The number codes for Greek; the Gnostic cosmology; the Pythagorean philosophical metaphors for the number series.

Key 8. Coptic—The number values for Coptic, derived from the Greek; Coptic astrological symbolism; the Egyptian hieroglyphs and their influence in the numbering of Hebrew and Greek.

Key 9. Runes—The ancient runic alphabet codes for Germanic, Icelandic, Scandinavian, and English Rune systems; the modern German Armanen Runic cult; the Irish Ogham and Beth-Luis-Nion poetic alphabets.

Key 10. Latin—Roman numerals as the first Latin code; the Lullian Latin Qabalah; the Germanic and Italian serial codes for Latin; the Renaissance cosmological model of three worlds.

Key 11. Enochian—The number codes for Enochian according to John Dee, S. L. MacGregor Mathers, and Aleister Crowley; the true pattern behind the Watchtower symbolism; the complete rectified Golden Dawn correspondences for the Enochian alphabet. **Key 12. Tarot**—The pictorial key to the Hebrew alphabet; the divinatory system for the Tarot; the two major Qabalistic codes for the Tarot emanating from France and England. **Key 13. English**—The serial order code for English; Aleister Crowley's attempt at an English Qabalah; the symbolism behind the shapes of the English alphabet letters.

The beauty of *The Key of it All* is that, although it deals with many foreign scripts, ancient tongues, and lost symbols, it is aimed at the beginning student. No previous knowledge of any of the languages is needed to appreciate and learn from this book. Everything that the reader needs is supplied within the text, including transliteration tables that convert all foreign scripts into English equivalents, copious introductory notes to each key, and an extensive annotated bibliography documenting all sources used in the text. If there is one book that captures every nuance of ancient number symbolism it is *The Key of it All*.

0-87542-318-3, 592 pgs., 7 x 10, illus., softcover   **$19.95**

COSMIC KEYS
Fortunetelling for Fun and Self-Discovery
by M. Blackerby
This book invites those just starting out in the psychic mysteries to jump in and take a revealing and positive look inside themselves and the people around them. Through the hands-on application of the Cosmic Keys—Chinese astrology (combined with Sun sign astrology), numerology, palmistry, card reading and finally, the author's original Dream Key and Universal Coloring Test—readers come away with telling insights into their individual personalities and life situations.The illustrations and coloring mantra were created especially for the workbook, and readers are encouraged to color each as they move through the book, as well as record personal data found in each section.

0-87542-027-3, 200 pgs., 7 X 10, illus., softcover   **$12.95**

NUMEROLOGY
The Universal Vibrations of Numbers
by Barbara Bishop

Numerology presents the easiest and fastest way yet to learn this ancient and amazing science. With your birth date, your given name (from your birth certificate), and this workbook, you can calculate and interpret your numerical vibrations and put them to use today. Through discovery of your vibrations, you gain the power to change any negative vibration to positive for a better way of life.

Simple, complete and efficient, this workbook/text enables you to discover your Universal Vibration and Personal Vibration digits that correspond to his or her life cycles, attainments and challenges.

Features of this workbook include: In-depth directions for constructing and converting numerology charts, Extensive work areas, Sample numerology charts, Blank numerology forms, Sample data sheets, Concise, easy-to-use appendices.

Who are you? Why are you here? Where are you going? Become actively involved in your own personal discovery with *Numerology: The Universal Vibrations of Numbers.*

0-87542-056-7, 224 pgs., 8 1/2 x 11, softcover $10.95

PALMASCOPE
The Instant Palm Reader
by Linda Domin

The road of your life is mapped out on the palm of your hand. When you know how to interpret the information, it is like seeing an aerial view of all the scenes of your life that you will travel. You will get candid, uplifting revelations about yourself: personality, childhood, career, finances, family, love life, talents and destiny. Author Linda Domin has upgraded and modernized the obsolete substance of palmistry. By decoding all the palm-lines systems of the major schools of palmistry and integrating them with her own findings, she has made it possible for anyone to assemble a palm reading that can be trusted for its accuracy.

This book was specifically designed to answer those personal questions unanswerable by conventional methods. Using this exciting method of self-discovery, you can now uncover your hidden feelings and unconscious needs as they are etched upon the palm of your hand.

0-87542-162-8, 256 pgs., 7 x 10, illus., softcover $12.95

Prices subject to change without notice.